David Mutschlecner

POETIC FAITH

THE LUNE

Poetic Faith: A Journal of Theopoetics

Revised Edition

ISBN 978-1-7328741-0-7

Library of Congress Control Number: 2018961918

Cover design by Indigo Deany

Printed in the United States of America

Published by

THE LUNE

Fort Collins, CO

www.poetsonearth.com

POETIC FAITH

PART ONE

PART TWO

I

Meditation

An experiment: sit in a field at the center of summer. Close your eyes and think of the radical contingency of your own flesh and blood existence. Now move outward in your mind, wheeling through every grass blade, every tree, every insect—the raven cry carries the expanding circle overhead — toward the encompassing hills, then out into the cobalt blue evening, then past that into night, deep space refulgent with points of sapphire. Wheel out through the galactic arms of the universe. Everything your mind touches upon contains *precisely* the same radical contingency that you found in your own heart. How does anything exist? A handful of primordial nothingness is cast like dust through every created thing. If this train of thought is tendentious, it can't be helped; you *feel*—this is not simply a philosophical experiment—by a dark and inexorable necessity. And yet this experiment should also bring you to a feeling of fearful reality, both of yourself and of everything else. The very notion that you are sustained at each moment by an infinite plenitude of all that is contingent means that this life that you call yours has value beyond finite conceiving; it means that every other life is subject to the same terms of wonder. *This is real; this is really happening. I am here by amazing grace and "marrow music,"* as Robert Duncan would say. The same mind that brought you to nothingness teems with sublime community.

2

Beauty

If poetry, as some critics say, is pure feeling, then it is feeling replete with intelligence, it is feeling that radiates thought. Parmenides, often called the father of metaphysics, wrote his philosophy, dictated by his Muse, *as poetry*. There are many examples of this sort in the history of poetry (Lucretius, Dante, Duncan, to name three more). In the end the poem is all mind. This does not mean the poem is all logic, or even full of clear thinking—beauty is far too great for our efforts, but beauty, in itself, is intellectually refulgent. I think Dante would agree with me.

Aquinas thought of beauty—because its keynotes are presumably order and proportion—as the divine formal cause of all things. I believe that beauty is rather the final cause of reality. Part of my reason for believing this is that we rarely read beauty with an easy eye or ear; and often when we do, what we are experiencing is not really beauty at all, but merely something comforting and nicely harmonized or balanced. We get flecks or flashes of beauty, but it is always too great for us to comprehend under the aspects of order and proportion. (I am reminded that Rilke, in his *Elegies*, wrote that beauty is the beginning of fear.) When we experience a radically new work of art, perhaps we have received a fleck of light from infinite beauty, and we cannot process it. Beauty draws all things, hence the reason it is so difficult, often, to understand, let alone define. Beauty is the breathing completion thought alone cannot complete.

3

Sign / Signified

Strong poetry frees an idea that may have been initially rooted by a specific meaning, to become something new. Let me give a personal example. The idea of the signified as living beneath the very skin of the sign is something I found in Thomas Aquinas' *Treatise on the Sacraments*. If the eucharistic host is the sign of Christ, then the signified—the real presence of Christ—is right there beneath the elevated sign. I don't have a desire to write a poetry dedicated to this kind of sacramental theology, but to *release* this realization of the sign/signified relationship, to let this idea go out into the world, seems a good thing to me.

This is a wish for poetry to confer its magic upon the world. From the well of words, as from a myriad of mouths, let the signified shine with new life. I do not leave theology behind so much as release it to become another thing. (In some way, words always wait for us to do this.) The theologian *as* theologian cannot do this. Where meaning is freed, meaning is at risk of loosing the parameters of dogma. This may be —for some—a fearful thing, but freeing meaning shows, in some manner, a kind of poetic faith. Poetic faith says that nothing of true value is ever lost, it is rather given new life. Truth rises as the light of language, deep from the well of words.

Dogmas fail when they try to equal the theophany they explicate. Any theophany is always greater than its description. The description lives only as a doorway back into the original theophany. Poets, when they are true to the Muse, know this inherently. A word does not so much point to a particular signified event or thing, it rather blooms with significant light that washes the whole landscape.

4

The Existential Plenum

Philosophic revelations are sometimes very quiet things, especially when they fall under the domain of metaphysics. Aristotle's shift from staid Platonic form to pliant potentiality was a quiet revolution that changed everything. Aquinas' shift from essence to existence was a similar revolution, but with, I believe, deeper implications. Every essence of every creature we can define is a mote of starlight awash in the great pouring plenum of existence, a plenum endless as Aristotle's sea of potentiality, but with this difference: existence, for Aquinas, is radiant with intelligence. This intelligence is a kind of light within light, a vision within every vision, an uncreated current beneath each creature. If *phronesis* is the working current, it gives birth to points of present-tenseness. Perhaps these are the essential points, the motes of essence, the mouths of words in the flood of light.

I rebel against any scientisim with a rigor equal to that which I level against the ossification of religious dogma. The dogmatist, be he religious or scientific, says with fervid avowal: *this is it, and this is all, there need be no further explanation of the territory we are examining.* This has a resonance of the rigor involved with Platonic forms. Forms were for Plato finite ideas; their perfection lay in their completeness, their finitude. With the shift from essence to existence as the first principal of metaphysics, we can say that there is always more. Always. Ideas, when they are good, lead into other ideas. Essences, if they are real at all, have porous skin — they breathe into each other. The plenum continues to pour, and we don't know what we will discover in it, but we do know that it will not, ever, be circumscribed by a finite idea. I speak this as a poet, which is to say I speak from the core of my own existence.

5

Metaphor

Metaphor is no mere trope, no simple subject of prosody. Metaphor is magisterial, essential. Metaphor is the pliant and unifying force, the active dynamism, involved in all the universe. The inherent similarity in dissimilars is that power whereupon creation acts, and that light whereby the mind understands creation. The important thing here is to see that metaphor is not a passive tool of thought, used in a craft work of poetry only to be put aside later. In metaphor we find the active self-revelation of being, for metaphor is that power of relationality through which things reveal themselves, and it is through metaphor's revelation that the mind knows itself.

Something becomes itself only in relationship with something else. A purely isolate being, excoriated of all relationship, is as close to nonbeing as we can get, for we have no thought of such a being. The *first* recognition of something— that it exists—is already a recognition rooted in relationship, because we are implicitly saying that this existing thing exists in a manner similar to other existing things. The object in question—whether an object of thought or a physical object—shares in the concept of existence. It is known, even at the implicit level of metaphysics, as being-in-relation. Everything in the universe inheres in everything else; everything has a share in the existential plenum.

Metaphor is not only a pairing of images, a smart overlapping of forms, it is rather a first cry that rises through the overlapping, for the first cry is like the curve of light, already turned toward unity. The communal cry is sexual and is unifying and is transcendent. You are swept up in the power of metaphor when, after a long day indoors, you go outside to see the vault of stars across the arc of darkness, and your vision soars upward to become one with the stars. This is a necessary verticality within the human person: the stars are who we are. Metaphor is not a confection of such relationship, it is the existential imperative of such relationship. You are *taken*, as Ganymede by Zeus, or Dante by Beatrice.

Neoplatonic philosophers will often talk about the self-diffusion of the good. By this they mean that the good, whether it be divine or creaturely must, by its very essence or definition, be an act of self emptying. When people talk of God, they often imagine this self emptying as from the top down. Given my star example, humans are often thought of as involved in a process of emptying that goes from the bottom up. If the universe is, as its definition suggests, turned toward unity, then self emptying is multidirectional, is holistic, is everywhere the fabric of life. The power involved in this weave is metaphor. The poet does not pull apart the threads to discover a static pattern and then imitate in her work such design. She lives in the unforeseen leaping of it. She is drawn by a dear imperative into its quick and thronging presence.

6

The Post-Historical Present

Twenty five years (or more) ago, the philosopher Arthur Danto developed the idea of the post-historical present. Danto's thoughts were devoted, primarily, to aesthetics. He felt that the history of western art was basically linear: one movement developed into another; one artist, or school of artists, found their energies by responding to what preceded them. The precedence lingered in their response. Advanced art moved through a fairly clear history, but always toward a new horizon. By the late fifties or early sixties, this history of art had reached its end. Contemporary artists who had an acute sense of their own present-tense-ness, no longer lived and worked on the old timeline. The post-historical present means that anything is possible, or perhaps more importantly: any combination of anything whatsoever, from any time, is available to the artist. The post-historical present sees, instead of a timeline, an oceanic sweep of plenitude moving in all directions.

Arthur Danto may have received the first inklings of his idea from Martin Heidegger who thought (perhaps a few decades prior to the fifties) that the history of philosophy was over. We live now in the fullness of philosophy, in the post-philosophic present. Heidegger felt that this end-of-philosophy wherein we live may be very long and very rich. We now can feel the presencing of things, the plethora of such verbal *presencing*, past philosophic categorization, past the dichotomization of reality. Heidegger tied this post-philosophic period with a pre-philosophic period. Being, as it offers itself in Heideggerian stillness, is ancient-new, or newly ancient. Philosophy has reached a kind of eschatological apex that is also a birthplace. We are experiencing the oldest birthplace of all, and yet it is our own birthplace. The voice of nowness is a primordial voice, and yet it is acutely ours.

Poetic faith says that within this voice we can find that anything—or any combination of things—is possible. Robert Creeley famously wrote: "Form is never more than an extension of content." Yes: we discover form in the going forth of the poem, measure bursts forth in manifold ways, but where does this form-going-forth come from? Surely, when we say with Pound, "Make it new," we are also saying: make it where it was first made. Make love where love was first made. Give yourself over to the energies of the poetic plenum. The Poem moves like a vast tide, rocking back and forth. Form is never more than a series of extensions of oceanic motion, crossing all time. Let these energies create you anew, let these powers write *you*.

7

Linger Awhile

For Heidegger, the verbal *presencing* of reality surrounds and includes both subjective and objective accounts of the world. Things *reveal* themselves, open themselves to us, if we are present *with* them. This is a very different sense of reality than what is offered through Aristotelian substance. With the notion of substance, Aristotle attempts to locate a strict objectivity, a made thing, enduring in its thingness. Though I believe that this search for a singular center that survives a lifetime of changes is, in itself, deeply mysterious and compelling, there are clear limits to what we can say about autonomous substance. *Presencing* surpasses the dichotomization of thing into substance and quality; it even slips through the relentless fixation of reality into cause and effect.

There is, after brief argument, a happy rapprochement between Aquinas' *esse* and Heidegger's *alethia*. Where *esse* is the act-of-being, *alethia* is the opening of a presence that reveals us as well. The offering of reality includes our eyes. *Action is the self revelation of being!* exclaimed the great contemporary Thomist Norris Clarke. Here is the essence of his book *Person and Being*: act-of-being = being-in-relation. Even breathing is such an act, revealing ourselves to others. Spirit is an inner dynamo, an energy source that reveals itself *in act*. What is revealed is revealed-in-relation.

Heidegger seems to be telling us to stay with things in the world longer than what may have been required by philosophic reason. Stay with the world awhile. Linger. Heidegger does not eschew causality, but he is wary of Thomism when, once we find the sufficient reason for any given creature in its ground, we pass the creature by, we put it away, so to speak: the effect is so blinded by cause that we no longer see, nor care to see, the effect at all. Thus the *presencing* of things slips through reason's hard dominion. Heidegger seems to be looking for that point where these two—cause and effect—are so intimate that the ground's giving birth is the ground's giving birth to itself. Stay with an object. Linger awhile till you see, in its quiet act-of-being, the ground itself revealed.

The poet lingers, not so much to produce a detailed description—this I believe is a misconstrued conception of poetry's function, a residue of some parsimonious analysis of substance. No: stay with something in order to see that whatever the signified may be, it pulses beneath a living sign.

8

Simplicity and Complexity

To hope means to change the meaning of the past, or to see a new meaning you did not see before. To see, in the gone-wrongness of it all, the seed of something new, is at once acutely human and acutely poetic. Wise Oedipus at Colonus is predicated upon the tragic Oedipus Rex. Beatrice, as the radiant union of love and intelligence, is predicated upon her untimely death. The poem of despair is a poem only despite itself; it was not aware of a secret thread in its own fabric. There is always something unforeseen in the weave, something only seen in retrospect. Perhaps this is the reason the muses are the daughters of memory. But they are not only this, they are memory brought forth into new actuation. Revision, when it is true, is new vision.

If I circumscribe myself by saying *I am this particular history of my life*, an interesting thing happens: the consciousness that allows for this closed circumscription is already, in its very thinking, larger than the harsh delineation just made. The definer mysteriously exceeds his self-definition, and he exceeds it in his very act of making it. The circumscription of my despair appears not to be entirely me. What is this larger life? We are left with hints and guesses. A simple oneness seems kenotically dissolved into everything. We think thoughts and yet we are not entirely one with the thoughts we think. Something surpasses the crazy mix, something like a breathing, expanding halo. God might say to the human person: *you are far more complicated than me, I AM infinitely simple.*

The saint's will is to be simple, but is it the poet's will as well? I don't know. The poet is beaten in the waves, the poet churns in the crazy mix, and yet all along she is aware of the halo—a pale blue light. The first and last poem are completely simple, and entirely free.

9

Relationship

Which comes first, substance or relationship? One cannot simply say substance, because everything seems predicated upon prior relationship. Even in some imagined initiatory state, we cannot ever separate being from relationship. Being grows from a ground of ceaseless interconnectedness, and this interconnectedness is logos itself, dreaming its own root and bloom.

In his *Treatise on Friendship* (from the *Summa Theologica*) Aquinas suggests that friendship is ultimately *not* necessary for happiness. What is necessary, in the end of ends, is the beatific vision, where we are suffused with the divine light that bears all love. Given his ground in a full Catholic ethos, Aquinas is technically right, but his answer seems weak to me in that it makes friendship accidental to happiness. It is as if Aquinas were saying: *of course friendship is important, but God alone is sufficient.* The answer feels uncomfortably incomplete. Whatever the beatific vision is, it *is* the communion of saints—the total interconnectedness of the human universe. This is not accidental to such vision—a kind of superfluous benefit, an added gift, as it were—it is essential, it is who we are in God. Further, I would say that the communion of saints is now, in any loving open conversation, any intimate, inclusive versing. These vital lines of friendship are the heart of theopoetics. I have come to see them as including the whole of creation.

Perhaps, in some act past all description, God is the spirit of relationship itself, perhaps God is the act—the *Esse*—of interconnectedness. In this sense *Esse* is and remains the ultimate mystery because it defies any definition. The strange thing about *Esse*, about existence itself, is that it fits under no genus, it slips through the limits of ideation. *Esse* is never substance, or essence, but is bright in the interstices between every being-in-relation. *Esse* is not sub-stance, but sun-stance. The light seeks free relaters, and its very seeking is at once an act of creation. Seeking and creating and relating are one divine verb. For the poet the Muse is this same spirit, seeking and creating poets as relaters. What is the poet but the catalyst for further relationships? The Muse wants us as sister muses.

10

"What Is A Poet—If Any Exists?"

There are perhaps only narrow windows in life where we meet our humanity, where we become, briefly, truly human. Even these windows may be less about realizing our humanity, and more about being made aware—as by a kind of shock —what full humanity *might* really mean. What is this meaning? It is difficult to say. It is what Dante tried to figure forth in his heaven-born neologism *trasumanar.* In a kind of holy paradox, paradise is that place where we are *trans-humanized* into our full humanity. At least, via Dante, we can imagine that the window is no longer narrow. We are in a state of complete relationality, a state exemplified by Karl Jaspers' concept of *Existenz.* When a person realizes herself as *Existenz,* she knows her entire being as a cipher for Transcendence. Everything is lifted, is offered up, through her person. She is the living symbol of all potential symbols. But Jaspers is always careful to pair *Existenz* with the word *possible.* We are *possible Existenz,* we are not yet fully human. Indeed, what is it to be *fully* anything? The window closes, and we sense that interior density again, that opacity: a place or anti-place beyond all communication.

William Carlos Williams wrote, somewhere in his late poetry: "Good Christ, what is / a poet—if any exists?" Full humanity and poetry are both understood provisionally. The poem, tight with its own self-conscious aesthetic, is no more poetry than is the man tightly involved with his own close-kept definitions. I take Williams' question very seriously: maybe there hasn't been a poet yet. Maybe we have gone through a few millenniums of trial and error. Maybe we have thought a lot without quite knowing what thinking is. Maybe full humanity is as fully a mystery as divinity. The poem begins where our humanity begins. Maybe we have, thus far, in all our great works, been given a mere inkling.

"A Felt Architectonics of the Numinous"

—Robert Duncan

Epic poetry of the Classic tradition kept its continuity through a mythic architectonics of deep power. Myth drove the inner dynamic of the poetry. Persons and events came to an epiphanic intensity because they were caught up in a greater cohesive play, a play that could change—we see this wonderfully in Aeschylus' *Oresteia*—but the pliancy is due to a mythic fabric that can still breathe. The charged numinous atmosphere surrounding the drama does not change. In Dante, narrative grew tall and strong through the nurturing atmosphere of a Catholic architectonics. It is important to recognize that this bright air is not the *same* as the going narrative, but it *allows* for the narrative to find its life. Problems, over the last hundred years or more, with long narrative poetry may therefore point to deeper conflicts that take us to the very horizon of our current struggle with meaning.

It is often insisted upon—perhaps too often and too insistently—that we now lack an overriding myth-structure to guide epic action in poetry. Pound, Williams, and Olson tried heroically. The saving grace of poetry is that, if they failed, their failures are part of the common consciousness of who we are. Seen in this larger context of our present struggle to find a lasting meaning, their giant poems don't really fail at all. Pound asked for direct treatment of the thing, whether objectively or subjectively considered. The clarity of this, of course, becomes quickly complicated.

Through his dictum, Pound would often flatten people into mere effigies of what he wanted. In postmodernism, direct treatment has been reduced to a kind of cool irony, if not sarcasm. I see no real reason to believe that this is direct treatment at all. There is a great overlap between Poundian imagism and Poundian vorticism. Once image becomes vortex for the in-rush of transhistorical ideas, once image becomes flame in a poetic rite of anamnesis, we are well past direct treatment. In his own way, Williams broaches the gap between historical reference, à la Pound, and living presentation. In *Patterson*, Williams' real power is as a kind of proto-conceptual poet, finding metaphor powerfully implicit in the lifted newspaper article. Olson found Nike alive in the streets of Gloucester. Clearly, neither Pound nor Williams nor Olson eschew numinous experience. There are powers at play in the mind and in the world, there is a kind of Hermes that holds the key to the hallway between them.

Numinous experience is hardly dead—it remains utterly endemic to the human person. We can color holy dread with sarcasm, we can deny that holy awe has any objective place, but such responses are shown for everyone, at one time or another, to be false. The world is full of gods, and the gods belie direct treatment unless direct treatment admits the full mysterious experience of being human.

A Theopoetics for Nishida Kitarō

What is poetry? I borrow from theology to seek a clearing in the question. Poetry is sought in the way of not knowing: the non-answer is *apophatic*. We look, and say: *it is nor this nor that*. It is not the line, at least not the line alone, nor image, solely, nor strictly intellect, nor even heart, for heart slips through its metaphors. All of these things remain pointers, ciphers, sources of symbol wherein vision soars toward a clearing in the question. But poetry is also *cataphatic*: it is all of the above and more and more. Since there is no autonomous essence to poetry—no self-involved inner ordering or form that stays the same forever—poetry can be everything. Poetry's self-emptiness is complete fullness. Poetry's pulse can be felt beyond all cogent understandings of the universe. There is always more.

I go a ways with the Japanese philosopher Nishida Kitarō. Poetry is less the synthesis, less the convergence of *apophatic* thesis and *cataphatic* antithesis, and more in the poise of lovingly holding the paradox in place. Poetry is both and not both, it is elsewhere, it is perpetually pointed to in the paradox of these polar points. It is in the not knowing that Hermes meets us. Surely this is like love. One loves without holding love securely in an object of knowing. The lover is endeared to certain qualities in the beloved, but these qualities are not the beloved herself. The mystery of love surpasses all tally, and is never simply a synthesis of all we know. Love exceeds both quantity and quality. Love holds the *apophatic* and *cataphatic* spirits in place as horizons of our very being. These spirits pass each other as on Jacob's angelic ladder, climbing up and down. They may even pass *through* each other, but in the end they do not blend. We go with the poetry of all we know, and all we do not know. Even the unknowing is love.

Both Aquinas and Kant posit powers within the mind, respectively the power of abstracting a universal from the singular, or the power of bequeathing an *a priori* idea to the phenomenological world. Nishida offers something very different from both of these options. Nishida is saying that consciousness *is* the continuity in discontinuity where subject and object continually trade places, and so in some way negate each other. Inside is outside and outside is in. The power of abstraction, or of an *a priori* idea, is in the quick of the poet's work.

The poet holds in creative tension subjective and objective accounts of the world. The self is resolved into its outer objects, and yet it is the ghost of the tally. To borrow from Nishida's phrase: there is finally no "object logic" to the mind. The self is subjectively held, and yet it is not so held. It is elsewhere, after the gem flashes and goes dark. It goes, in the bright acknowledgment before death. In the dark the poem goes on, into the ultimate paradox of God that seems to hold everything so infinitely that She would be nothing of anything. And yet, as we uncover our own nothingness, in some wild, unforeseen way, we enter God, and know where we have always been.

What is poetry? It is a grace of bewilderment where subjective and objective calls become a sometime cacophony. What do we see and hear? The answer becomes a complex of awe-full contradictions where object logic fails us. According to Nishida, we understand the object when we in some way *become* the object, even as we remain ourselves. He insists that this is as much true for the scientist as it is for the artist. The idea is perhaps the deepest root of all philosophy; it goes from the pre-Socratics through Aquinas—it is a kind of alpha and omega. In the moral sphere, becoming the object is what allows for compassion and thus gives birth to a numinous reverence that can take in the world. Were we truly and strictly creatures of object logic, knowing the world without any need of our personal selves, there would be no compassion, no fellow-feeling, and hence no spirituality, and thus no humanity.

These days I feel the measure of my poetic climb has flatlined. Thought has been weighted away from whatever of perception's peak I thought to find. But I was told, late at night and alone, as if by a voice not mine, that God does not dichotomize the human universe into horizontality and verticality, anymore than he does into subjective and objective positions. To be squat down in the quotidian may be for God an entirely different matter than I can imagine. We do not know what kind of psychic terrain God sees. The data is different when the mind is all eye.

Dōgen, a near contemporary of Aquinas, wrote:

> One who falls to the ground
> uses the sky to stand up
>
> One who falls to the sky
> uses the ground to stand up

In this he rhymes with his later counterpart, Nishida Kitarō: "True self identity is not A is A, as is usually thought, but rather a unity of contradictions." A grace of bewilderment.

What is poetry? Holy vortex of the question.

13

Toward a Redefinition of Metaphysical Poetry

Radical embrace is instantiated in radical contingency. There is an at-once-ness to this that makes metaphysics essential to poetry.

The power of physics comes from measurement; its quantitative sophistications stride with stars and creep with quarks. Metaphysics is qualitative, it seeks the mystery of essence—the active mystery of what most vitally informs the world. Where a quantitative approach leads to praxis, a qualitative approach leads to meaning. Meaning is being, first and last: the basic good of existence itself. Every being's meaning is predicated upon a more inclusive meaning. This is as much as to say that there is nothing, nothing at all in the whole universe, that is not contingent upon something else. Nothing contains the necessary reason for its own existence. No creature can say: *I simply am and always have been and always will be—I rely solely and strictly upon my own vitality. I lift myself up by my own bootstraps.* Because nothing can say this definitively, everything is in radical embrace with everything else. The mystery of vitality is the mystery of community is the mystery of commonality is the mystery of poetry.

In this explication, I am not being religious, I am being common. I am basic being at this beer-stained table top, writing as I can. Radical embrace is neediness and love, it says I can't go it alone—I am hopelessly contingent. In poetry this contingency marks the existential marriage of ecopoetics and theopoetics. Here is a possible equation:

ecopoetics : radical contingency :: theopoetics : radical embrace

Or maybe it is the reverse. In any case we are in an urgent domain, and where this urgency addresses me I know the voice of the Muse—I am at once in the heart of metaphysics and in the heart of poetry.

14

Poetic Language

Broadly speaking, there are perhaps two ways of approaching language in poetry. The first way is that of seeing words as the melopoetic vehicle, the well-constructed Apollonian chariot bearing the Sun (logopoeia) across the blue arc of the sky (phanopoeia). The second general approach to poetic language—which happens to be my own—is where the sun-source is the chariot itself: the scored words are the source of their own meaning. The chariot of words does not *carry* the sun-meaning of logopoeia, it *is already* the bright meaning itself. The chariot still charts the arc of phanopoeia, but its proclamation is less a description *of* the sky, and more a sing-ing *to* the sky, to the whole theatre of the world. The chariot does not so much trace the sensorium, but the sensorium sings through the chariot's light.

Words are the poem's sun-source. Words both carry and create a cosmology. The sun is the wheeling story.

Listening

Logopoeia is born out of melopoeia—this, for me, is a truth of poetic faith. When a poet pays close attention to how vowels and consonants *sound*, one against another, she is, at the same time, witnessing birth from the well of meaning. "Music-magic," to borrow a phrase from Robert Duncan, becomes meaning-magic. It is as if, in the auditory love-making of assonance and consonance, a penumbral logos is released—a light from sound. In the friction of two T sounds — *fleet/cut*—there is a flash point. In the lapping of two L sounds (right there!) the moon washes in. The sounded O ought always to open us up.

I am not sure if a poet can purely begin with logopoeia and then reach melopoeia. One can begin, of course, with a philosophical idea, but the idea may not be able to self-consciously confect its own sculptural sound. Sound must find the idea hiding in the secret ocean of its shell-like ear. Sound must delight in the idea, and curl about it like a tongue. I have a markedly incomplete idea of how this works, but the mystery of poetic faith claims that it does indeed work. Music-magic gives birth to meaning-magic. When a meaning overcomes us, it can be comprehended only as music. We are in thrall to the one as to the other. I believe this is true even in the case of someone as logical as Aquinas—the logic only takes us to the edge of the trans-logical, whose melody washes back over every rigor that came before.

16

The Existential Angel

Platonic form is a blazing angelic presence. The angel does not evolve—the form is terrifyingly complete. Angelic utterance is replete in its first communication, there is no emendation, no hint of a change of mind. Even if what the angel tells us is partial, it comes from an already complete revelation—a bright arc under whose finish we are blinded. The human quotidian, made up of change and duration, is frightened by this timeless, finished rigor. We speak in trembling partialities, our touch is earthen, breaks and flows as earth breaks and flows.

Great poetry has always sought to reconcile these two currents of intelligence, it has even sought to see how the one is only grasped in the other—the verdant created world in the golden uncreated realm, uncreated mind in sensual creation. Doesn't contemporary poetry still need the Fire in the fire, the unchanging *I AM* in the burning desert of our lives? Isn't this ancient alchemical work of turning the existential and the Platonic into each other, of coming, in the turning, to a new epiphany, still our work? My poetic faith says that this is the end and beginning of all creative thinking, from Dante to Dickinson and back again. We shall forever seek the existential angel.

Striding

Let me figure forth a kind of peripatetic epistemology first suggested by Kazuaki Tanahashi in his study of the *Heart Sutra*. With one leg we place the weight of thinking upon the world of plurality: each leaf is different, everything is unique and precisely itself. With the other leg we place the epistemic weight upon the oneness of all things: creation is a unity, there is one shared life—interconnection is every-thing. By these two legs we walk, and so think. Our con-ceiving of the world is a walking in the world. We need both legs in order to do so. Both ways of thinking are harmonized in one cognitive body. Were we to have only one of the two epistemic appendages, our thinking, our very perceiving, would be crippled and incomplete.

"Form is emptiness and emptiness is form," the *Heart Sutra* famously proclaims. I take form, by my own Aristotelian inclinations, to be the principle of individuality, and hence of multiplicity—manifold form gives birth to the crazy wave of all things. Emptiness is the principal of unity—the wave nature of matter itself, slipping through every thought, through every attempted formal delineation.

How is form emptiness, and emptiness form? Well, let us take a given *in-formed* substance, sitting on your table top. Bread is bread because it is in-formed by farmer and baker and so their extended families, and so—by necessary consequence—the whole world of humanity. Bread is bread because it is grain and so world, and so—by necessary con-sequence—the entire cosmos conspires to be the warm loaf resting on your table. The form of bread is empty so that the form of bread can be full. To know this negating of autonomous substance (Aristotle's sense of form) leads to a complete affirmation of all that life offers us.

In our epistemic stride between the one and the many, mind must be present in order to find the shifts in perception meaningful. My slice of bread is not your slice of bread, and yet the cosmos is one loaf. Mind is the mystery, kneaded into the mix, the no-thing that leads to all that is distinctive. Mind is the needy seeing that everything seen needs. Mind is the striding poem, the striding, stirring poem.

Thanksgiving

The inception of philosophy is wonder, a "wonder-struck beholding," as Hannah Arendt so beautifully puts it. Wonder curves as a rainbow of overriding consequence—a light that connects earth and sky. Wonder is always close to something like a theophany, an awe filled thanksgiving, kindred both to fear and praise.

Being and the thought of Being are One. This is the divine beginning place of Father Parmenides. The same primordial first-last Genius informs both thought and cosmos. Heidegger profoundly added to this when he said that to *think* and to *thank* are essentially the same; they come from the same etymological root. This means, wonderfully, that creation is a continual offering up of thanksgiving; creation itself is quintessential eucharist! The body of all being is forever given as it is forever truly thought, and all thought is the same offering forth of itself. Thought-thinking-itself is this inclusive Praise-Wonder—a cosmos of nothing but poetry.

The Child of the Universe

Didn't Augustine write somewhere that God is the youngest one of all? Poetry flares from what Robert Duncan called "Promethean infancy." The God of the spark is alive in each one of us, especially when we take redemptive risks, where life saved is life sacrificed, immolated so that the fire goes on, the passion plays through. Poetry is relentlessly transcendent and passionately inclusive. The transcendence I write of is not a leaving behind of anything, but an intensification of everything. Passionate inclusion occurs through this very intensification. This is the fiery vision I need. The Promethean child transcends in her risk taking play because her drama is the drama of all things. All things become intensely themselves in redemptive youthful love. The Promethean child tenders the ember which, while being most assuredly hers, belongs to all things. Her auguries come from the whole and return to the whole.

Here is Robert Duncan:

> Do you come from my heart,
> sweet penetrating drum?

> (...)

> No, Beloved Sleeper, the beat you hear
> repeats in the awakening of all hearts
> the seed of a fire in the heart of What Is

The Copula

If I create a simple sentence of subject-copula-predicate, such as: *Oedipus is king*, I can either take the copula as pointing toward the quality of kingship, or pointing back toward Oedipus himself. If the *isness* of Oedipus is always predicated upon accomplishment, then we can see him only as king, or only as guilty of incest and patricide. It is only when the fundamental *isness* of Oedipus is not entirely sucked into these predications, but is realized as the mysterious well of personhood, that we come to see him as he is known at Colonus. In the well of his own unqualified being, Oedipus is recognized as a sacred person, blessing the ground he is found resting upon.

This is not so difficult a thing to perceive. The pliant spirit and pure beauty of a child is loved, not because of any accomplishment (the predications attached to the given child) but because of her clear springing *isness*, the act-of-being, the priceless is of who she is. It is impossible to overestimate how important this is for society at large. A person is not sacred because he swells with accomplishment, a person is sacred because he is a person. Any homeless man might be Oedipus at Colonus, blind and seeing and feeling the earth, the temple being present where ever he walks or rests. Contrary to this, any powerful political figure might be Oedipus Rex, ready to be brought down through his own heavy hubris.

Acquired accomplishment only becomes relational—and hence of sacred value—when the copula roots back into personhood. When any Oedipus recognizes that he simply *is*, he has found, simultaneously, that his *isness* roots into the interconnective *Is* of all existence. The simple *is* of any of us, when it is cupped and loved, becomes the inclusive *Is* of all of us. When Ezra Pound in a cage at Pisa (his own Colonus) bends down and places his hands upon the ground, he surpasses the heavy predication, or qualification, of the *Cantos*.

Some people, especially some of the smartest people, never get to this basic existential spring-source. To say that something exists means almost nothing to them because the only *something* is the *whatness* of anything. In other words: the subject is sucked entirely into the predicate. The *is* is only an arrow that points to the predicate, and if the *whatness* of the predicate appears to be valueless, then the subject is also valueless. The wonder of existence—which is purely given — is not, in itself, very interesting to them.

The poet cups the blue flame of the *Is*, and knows this simple and inclusive miracle as an ever returning epiphany, the proem and coda of an ever opening Voice. The poet is homeless because this epiphany forever exceeds the world's tally. The poet is not, in the end, terribly interested in what the civilized (and popular and smart and monied) world has to offer. She is a citizen of heaven. Where she rests she finds that the temple rests with her.

Robert Duncan

In Canto 33 of the *Purgatorio*, Dante's Pilgrim crosses the rivers Lethe and Eunoe. Lethe washes away all the bitter memories that life incurs. The baptism of Eunoe returns all the good things done, and the good things received, back to consciousness. In his wonderful late poem "The Quotidian," Robert Duncan proclaims the Lethe he experiences as not simply an allusion to classical poetry. Lethe is a reality of life; it is a river he is really passing through.

This is a tremendously important aspect of Duncan's poetics. When the poet calls forth such an allusion as Lethe, or such mythical gods as, say, Venus or Athena, he is calling forth, and consequently experiencing, real presences, real powers we have, in the course of poetry's history, ascribed with multiple names. These names are mouths wherethrough real presences arise into the poem. The poet does not *allude* to classical poetry—this would be a show of surface erudition or mere witticism. No: the poem as an act-of-being is a real experience of these presences, a real return to, and carrying of, these felt powers. Whatever names we give to these powers, they are indeed actualities. And it is through them that the poem, itself, is found to be a palpable actuality. The poem, for Robert Duncan, is always the real thing.

The Icon

The human face is an icon before the face is painted. The eyes are already a window into eternity. Human hands are sacred before they make sacred any religious object. The human voice, before it issues words of consecration, is already consecrated to a holy order consubstantial with creation itself.

The sabbath, Jesus said, is for the human person, not the human person for the sabbath. Sacred things are sacred insofar as they have a sanctifying effect upon us. When a religious object is closed off in its own untouchable sanctity, pietism has appeared. I do not object at all to things set aside for a holy purpose, but this purpose ought to be efficacious in opening windows onto the shared mystery of humanity and divinity. I do not object to poetry made for a holy purpose. It could be argued that all great poetry is made in the spirit of transcendence. When a poem lives and breathes in an act of inclusive transcendence—when, in whatever manner, the offering up includes us—the poem has indeed been made for a holy purpose.

Poetry is the expanding circumference wherethrough the divine center finds its meaning amplified. Poetry is the face of the mandala, and the mandala as icon—a kaleidoscope of eyes into eyes, and a wide blue light beyond them.

II

I

Kenosis

Sacred kenosis—the self-emptying of God that makes creation a sensual reality—takes on, via the Vedas, a mythical configuration. There is an almost Orphean picture of divinity at work here:

> Not having anything out of which to create the world,
> he has to resort to himself, dismembering himself,
> offering himself as a sacrifice, falling into pieces so that
> life is drained from him.

> (Panikkar, *The Vedic Experience*)

Orpheus is dismembered—and the rending is not without violence—so that river and wind can sing, everywhere, with a divine voice. This mythical kenosis is wonderfully striking. God's body becomes the limbs, the supports, of the world's body. The sacrifice is real, and complete. God-for-us takes on a new and startling meaning. God's dismemberment, Her singing immanence, is Her All, and if we are to find this holy All—or immanent awe—it must be here or nowhere, because the nowhere of divine deeps—uncreated being in itself—is not known, not placed, not given to eyes nor hands nor ears.

According to the Vedas, God's kenotic act is so extreme that Her poured out being is helpless; She is at risk of loosing Her original integrated depth. She is scattered through the cosmos — through all religious reifications of the cosmos. Transcendence is inculcated into immanence to the point of helplessness (a helplessness not unlike that of Jesus on the cross).

Creation, turned away from the gushing depth of divine immanence, looses its own deeps. But, according to the Vedas, the primordial waters, the first-born of God, sing back to Her, and so reclaim the divine deeps as their own true being. How different a picture this is from Thomistic omnipotence, where creation must, by logical necessity, remain inessential to God, for if creation was essential to God then something would be lacking in Her being; She would have a need for the sensual world. In the Vedas, God wheels "with rocks and stones and trees," as Wordsworth would put it. This marks the great Paschalian fear—the cosmic gulf of uninhabited spaces where the very spirit of things seems helpless and alone. Our humanity lives in an act of kenosis, a god-act coextensive with the divine outpouring of everything, or else humanity, quite simply and frightfully, does not come to be.

How do we come to be? Perhaps the artist knows something of this, because the artist is always beginning again, and is not afraid of failure. Perpetual kenosis is perpetual beginning, and dismemberment is inceptive shaping. Scattering: inceptive gathering. The break up and break down of the poem that is so acutely felt *right now* may be this very necessary beginning. The poem is being rent in the roil of what the world has become. Still, the poem will not betray us. We shall discover ourselves in the torn cloth where, as Robert Duncan so marvelously put it, "we reaving" becomes "re-weaving."

2

Parmenides / Paul

Being and the thought of being are one—so Parmenides famously channels his Muse. It is utterly vital to realize that this *credo*, if you will, carries an existential shock similar to that Saul experienced when being thrown off the high horse of his orthodoxy. Parmenides realized, in what for him was the pivotal moment of his life, that we are not simply thinking beings, rather we are *Thinking-Being*, we are the consciousness of one totality. From this I see acutely that the birthplace of metaphysics is endemically mystical—non-dualistic, transcendent, and essentially advaitic. I find this to be of immense importance for the very idea of thinking.

When, in the book of *Acts*, Saul was thrown off his horse, he heard the Christ-Voice say: *Saul, Saul, why do you persecute me?* He had in fact been persecuting the first followers of Jesus. The body of Christ, as he later called it, was essentially the collective body of these people. It was the shock of this revelation that turned Saul to Paul. Let me attempt a philosophic connection between this Paulist shock and the life-changing epiphany of Parmenides. Just as Parmenides had the heady sudden understanding that we are *Thinking-Being*, holding Being's radiant body—at least virtually—within our consciousness, so Paul realized that all creation weeps and suffers toward one inclusive Body. The limbs and supports are scattered, but there is an inclusive unity in mind, and this unity shimmers like a memory upon the waters of creation. I know this relationship I am making between Paul and Parmenides is, theologically at least, at best tenuous, but philosophically they are related because both come from a shock to the whole thinking system. Both Parmenides and Paul say: *there is a present-absent-present with which I am intimately connected. I am dispersed and gathered within this unity, just as the divine is dispersed and then recalled to itself through the love of its scattered members.* These scattered members—even ourselves!—are the Vedic limbs that support the cosmos through their sacrifice and praise. Thinking-Being is an act of transcendent-encompassing. We transcend only by holding tenderly all that the world offers us, *in body.* This body is both mind and matter, suffused with one another.

It is precisely faith that makes thinking possible,
for faith offers the unthought ground out of which
thinking can emerge

(Panikkar: *The Vedic Experience*)

How does this "unthought ground" relate to Parmenidean Thinking-Being? Unthought ground sounds passive, without energy, but I don't think it is. This ground marks a passionate imperative, which is the Ur-Word, the unspoken that is offered as spoken words, and can only be offered in the faith that there is, indeed, a connection between this unspoken imperative and what we speak out. The unthought ground, the Urgent-Unspoken, is the Being that is one with the thought of Being. And the quick arc between these two, the blue spark, is faith.

To give without faith is merely an attempt to give without connection to this word-incipient ground; it would be to give as if from the ground of your own isolate self—as if this were even possible. The Body of Christ for Paul was this given ground of Being—the creative engendering Word of All. Orthodoxy had come to mean for Saul order and law that stood in isolate rigor—rootless in sheer rigor—enacted without thought addressing the inclusive Body. When Saul became Paul, he began to think from this Body—Being and the thought of Being became one.

3

A Poetics of Gender

The idea that the human person is capable of becoming anything, that her embrace is virtually infinite, leads to the radical freedom of early existentialism. This idea did not find its birthplace in the twentieth century. Aquinas says much the same thing. The difference, for us, is really one of intensification. Raimon Panikkar writes that our form—or soul, if you will—*is* this very openness to all.

> We do not have any fixed nature, nor are we a fixed nature. Our only nature is that we can become everything.

> (Panikkar, *The Rhythm of Being*)

This is the fearful Sartrean freedom reinserted into a text on natural theology where the image of God *is* openness, an openness intimately and radically connected with every other open thing in the universe.

That the Catholic faith holds in large part this view of the human soul is interesting to me because, at the same time, Catholicism denies this openness when it comes to gender. What I hear is something like this: *Yes, we can be all that there is in the universe except with regard to gender, where each person remains rigidly male or female. There is no gender fluidity, there is no becomingness when it comes to gender.* It seems to me that humanity and history simply belie this.

Poetry belies this. The fluidity of the poem is one with the fluidity of gender. I wrote in my poem:

> The man in the moon in the woman whose moon
> is penumbral inclusion

The strength of anything is lost when we grasp it too hard. To transcend through any power within us, the power must be free to become whatever it wants. For the poet, the symbolic image itself becomes streaming, fluid. Gender as the mark of our humanity can do no less. The hallways inside us are streaming and fluid. Images (and all images are in some way images of ourselves) are rivers. Gender cannot escape being a part of this. I am a man and a woman. I am the seasons mixed. In the reach of the holy poem, I am Persephone and Pluto, I am Cupid and Psyche. I am Beatrice, transgendered.

Gender is a work of streaming divine imagination as much as it is of biology; indeed biology is subject to this pliant divine work. It is sadly absurd that the Roman Catholic hierarchy still insists that women cannot be priests, and that LGBT people cannot love and marry whom they choose. I pity Catholic intellectuals who spend their energies trying to honor the stricture of their religious law while at the same time trying to find a way through this law in order to honor people as they are. I hear much about *a softening of tone*— some mollified form of gratification. This kind of thing is exhausting and fruitless. The paradigm needs to change; deeper imperatives need to be attended to.

4

Advaitic Existenz

The more we learn about matter, the more we learn about the holes or spaces within matter. Absence seems to expand exponentially with every small understanding of presence. The spaces in our understanding seem to grow and grow with every little patch of knowledge. This may be a frustration to the cosmologist who seeks a total and complete world-picture, who wants an "explanation of everything," but to the poet emptiness is in felt apposition to freedom. Space is the breath of the poem. Where breath is spirit, energy is the line that the breath consumes, and then releases to become, again, space for another line. So the lines of the poem are the food of the spirit. We will not reach the end of this process; even death, our own death, is a part of it.

To think Being, in a Parmenidean way, does not mean thinking of an explanation of everything. It means rather being free in the whole, which as whole forever eludes us, expands past us. The whole is the field of the poem's celebration. The whole makes the poem possible. Spirit consumes and releases poem within poem. Existenz, for Karl Jaspers, is the free vision of an ever-expansive totality. The advaitic will to unity—eschewing mere explanations and ridged dichotomies—is the out-reach and in-reach of spiritual breath. Advaitic-Existenz admits uncertainty, and is free even in uncertainty. It is only in this breathing conception that we are what Parmenides might call *Thinking-Being*.

From Dante's Valley of the Kings

Rae Armantrout needs Robert Penn Warren

John Berryman needs Robert Creeley

John Milton needs Alice Notley

Louise Gluck needs Dan Farrell

Allen Tate needs Allen Ginsberg

James Merrill needs Lyn Hejinian

Gerard Hopkins needs Walt Whitman

Edmund Spenser needs Cid Corman

Gary Snyder needs W. H. Auden

Geoffery Hill needs Frank Samperi

Harold Bloom needs David Antin

Robert Lowell needs Robert Lax

Robert Frost needs Louis Zukofsky

Susan Howe needs Ivor Winters

Charles Olson needs Shakespeare

These are rhymes of redemption. Let our attentions bear forth such transformative power.

6

The Fractal Poem

Just as the leaf repeats the tree, just as the rose window is both microcosm and macrocosm, so spirituality itself has a fractal nature. This is Perry Schmidt-Leukel's wonderful suggestion at the end of his 2015 Gifford lectures. There are religious proclivities that repeat themselves across the spectrum of human experience. Devotion, law, and mystical leanings lead us everywhere. Might we say that these proclivities are seeded by God? If so, then how does God use them? Perhaps — in a kind of epiphanic consciousness—God meets God at the spark-point of these proclivities. I am reminded that religion, despite the blood-bath of its history, means literally to reattach the ligament (*relagare*). Religion was meant to mend the cord that connects us to one another. The divine becomes lovingly manifest in this reattachment; God again knows herself in us. These repeating connections, or possible connections, bear a theophanic light, reflected fractally. There is a patterning to love as it expands.

These are issues of the morning of our nativity; this is the dawning of the poem. Of course this poem quickly becomes a struggle, but it can be a loving struggle. "The Law I Love is Major Mover," writes Robert Duncan. I could let any law in myself become hegemonically ossified. But if the law is Major Mover, I can work to see in myself where such law flames up as other-directed devotion. The law that I love my neighbor as myself is inherently trans-dualistic, and hence advaitic, and hence mystical. The Major Mover in me is seeded with deeper mysteries. Devotion, law, and mystery: even within myself these spiritual dimensions are fractal, and foment one another.

A fractal spiral runs through the eye of our needle and
expands on both sides into a vast cosmic coil, a sidereal
vortex. Any image may be the eye of the needle: the fleck of
a crystal, a snowflake. The lens whereby we see is in anyone's eye. The peacock's tail-feathers flare across the night.
And in the poem, each word is an opening in sight.

7

Robert Lax

Robert Lax wrote lines of pure verticality, up and down the page. In one poem he wrote *is* thirty-three times: three groups of seven and two groups of three. Like this:

is
is
is
is
is
is
is

The careful sewn seam of existence. One senses the thread going prayerfully in and out. Where do we find this fine stitch-work? In the fiber of every grass blade. In the unfolding of every leaf in the mind. In the still consciousness of every tree limb as it lifts and divides. In the sheer verticality of the highest twigs. In another poem Lax suggests that the most beautiful thing in art is the straight line, but that each point of this line is a flower. Each needle-point of the stitch-work is a microcosmic bloom.

Elsewhere, Lax writes that the great arms of the setting sun spread upon the waves and quiet them. So the seam is fluid, and runs on the waters, and runs in our blood. What was vertical is now horizontal; it is all the same line seen with different eyes. It is all *Is*. Lax watches as wing-shadow soars horizontally against a soaring wall. Up-surge is a power everywhere felt.

There is one star for each silver needle-point. Each thread-point is a poem, but in the end, Lax marvelously writes, there is only one star, only one poem—one long poem we all participate in, small as a syllable and great as the cosmos. How often, when Lax breaks his verticals of words into syllables, we come upon onomatopoeia: the cry of *ow* or simply *o*. These are the breath-exclamations of all of us. Lax says that when we breathe in and out we are rowing. The quick-silver sapiential seams in our wake come from the efforts of our breath. We are rowing. Our lives are, alternately, a weak or a strong pull, and the *o* we breathe in and out is the sun and the moon over the water. Both the sun and the moon are at once, given and received in respiration. So the straight lines finally form a great circumference, a circle of light. As with Nicholas of Cusa's "coincidence of opposites," straight becomes curved and curved becomes straight. In the summer storm, Lax writes, one child cries *fire*, while the other (her brother) cries *water*. Both are right.

There is always more silence than wind, and always more wind than silence. There are more words than letters; there are more letters than words. The beautiful and powerful (and humble) thing about Robert Lax, is that he shows us how, in breaking word-things down into syllable-things, we come upon countless riches, countless possibilities—more wealth than can be contained in all the volumes of the world.

> Trans
> lu
> cent

A particle of light becomes a penny, a cent, a little coppery circle, a small flower—it is all we need to pay our way.

A penny for your thoughts—a cent or a sense—for the full arc of the voyage. A little poem that becomes a great conversation.

8

Creation - vs - Confection
Ends - vs - Means

In his *Metaphysic of Morals*, Kant came, rather fortuitously, upon the lasting truth that persons are sacred ends in themselves, and never a mere means to some other end. Needless to say, history shows us the seemingly endless tragedy of what happens when persons are taken as mere means. That Kant came—almost stumbled—upon this truth is worth noting. The truth was not a confection of his critique, but seemed purely given, indeed seemed to *break* in upon his linked thinking from eternal consciousness itself.

I think there is an important distinction to be made here between creation and confection. In the huge confection of Citizens United, we see the idea of persons distorted. When the corporation becomes a person then real flesh and blood persons again become mere means for the accrual of close-kept money. In a plutocracy the person becomes a mere means for the wealth of a few. The spiritualization of capitalism—held by some politicians on the far right—seems to me to be deeply wrong-headed. The idea that people, in such a vision of capitalism, will naturally fall or rise to the level that is right for them, is insidious. I have known far too many working class people who have been thwarted in their talents by lack of money, or lack of time to do much of anything else but work, or through the nets of familial or personal tragedy. Their dreams cannot take shape, and by middle age they simply give up. There are many people like this. The far right does not do the work of creation, but the faux work of confection. My response to them is that I need to find some other way whereby love might break through the links of their chain.

I pay close attention to what happens in the poem. When something breaks in, when something is purely given, as from eternity, I feel a way has been found, at least for the time my wandering mind can attend to it. When I want (or even insist) that the poem continue, when my desire is that the links keep being made, then the long poem becomes confected. It is at this point that the door to ongoing creation seems to close.

When was Ezra Pound open to creation, and when was he involved in the itch of confection? One might study *The Cantos* with this question as a light upon the page. The long open-ended poem remains an ideal for me, but it is ideal-as-end, as sacred end. Each part of the poem must also be an end-in-itself. Each phrase must speak openly, right where it is, as a person with her words. There is a kind of creative metonymy at work here. The difference between the poem as metaphor for person, and the corporation as person, is that the former perforce pours forth its life—indeed, if the poem is valid at all, its life is this pouring forth—while the latter is merely a legally bound fabrication that trickles at best.

The long poem is a bit like justice, which we labor for, but which has its own epiphanic moments, its own fortuitous showings. In such showings we see people revealed as people, full of goodness and errors. (Pound's poem is revealed, in various instances, as both good and horrible.) Poetry, to borrow from Kant again, vitally roots back to the *noumenon* of its flaring epiphanic moment. The *phenomena* of its sonorous manifestation is in the ear. I need to listen while

I write, I need to pay attention to the unfolding measures of thought itself. I also need to yield, to open up places wherein eternity might enter.

9

A Theopoetics for Raimon Pannikar

Homeomorphic equivalency: what is out-formed pluralistically comes from some same-shaped mystery, some under-shape, Ur-shape of the Holy. There is overlap in our theological shape-shiftings. Different reckonings of God cross paths as we try to parse out how the divine intercuts creation.

Homeomorphic equivalency becomes a real challenge when dealing with such seemingly disparate concepts as *sunyata* (Buddhist radical emptiness) and *pleroma* (Christian fullness and completeness). Raimon Panikkar expresses the belief that compassion for all creatures only comes when one experiences the complete emptiness of all created things. *Pleroma* only comes through *sunyata*. This is a holy paradox that I cannot pretend to have realized. I make some approach toward understanding when I see that compassion is proportionate to self-emptying—this is to measure and test the paradox within myself. I take seriously Panikkar's avowal that inter-faith communication goes hand-in-hand with *intra*-faith thinking. To have inter-faith versing among a company of poets, I need to have an inner-versing within myself. The argument with others is an argument within myself; the accord with others is accord within myself.

With intra-faith communication I start to get a sense of the homeomorphic equivalency beneath sunyata and pleroma. Fullness may be emptiness seen inside out. Emptiness may be the always more of complete fullness—the vast cup—or the myriad cups—of creation wherein pleroma's wine is poured and poured. I know that something must give way

—the seal of selfhood must be drawn off for the wine to go in —but I also know there must be a cup before any wine can be poured. What is the cup? What is personhood? This remains an unfathomable mystery. I might say it is fathomed only by the wine, but then the wine is only shaped by the cup. So then indeed between the wine (*pleroma*) and the cup (*sunyata*) there is a homeomorphic equivalency, but what this *same-shape* is remains an enigma. It seems only known in the bringing together of emptiness and fullness. I am tempted to say that it doesn't exist *without* this bringing-together.

All of this is intra-faith communication, a conversation within myself, but with inter-faith meeting it is repeated. So a poetic rhythm is created, where inner measure meets outer measure. This kind of exchange goes on and on. I read this exchange as I read everything. In the end (or in the beginning) to read silently is to read aloud. Creation is listening. Or rather: creation is reading with me.

Qualified Tautologies

If both Creator and creation are real to me, then I might say they both have real being, but if being circumscribes both Creator and creation, then I have caused a philosophical problem for myself: now being itself seems greater than its two parts. To get around this problem, I say that God *is* being, but now there is another problem: if God is the totality then creation must somehow be a part of God. Creation is an expansive unfolding; creation marks the history of being. Being is becoming and becoming is being. What is there outside of this tautology that might illuminate its two points?

Again: I might pretend to get past the subject/object dichotomy, but then *something* gets past this dichotomy. I might profoundly fool myself and say I no longer *have* consciousness, but am consciousness itself, a kind of inclusive cosmic consciousness, like the Hindu Brahman, but if this breakthrough is mine, then I again have a consciousness of it. Subject (or self) is predicated upon object, and the great object, the totality if you will, is predicated upon the conceiving subject. I cannot get outside the polar points to explicate them further.

Again: Transcendence makes no sense without immanence. There must be an immanent ground of language, of the world configured within us, that is lifted up and made bright with meaning. Transcendence is immanence and immanence is transcendence. The philosophical problem is that there is no light or space outside of the tautology. It is like trying to conceive a space outside of cosmos, even as we know that cosmos is internally contingent.

What is a problem for philosophy is not a problem for poetry. Poetic faith is in the tautology, the holy equivalency. Poetry is not trying to solve a problem, but it does try to shine a light into philosophy, a light wherein the problem does not disappear but is rather transformed. Poetic faith feeds a qualified tautology, an equivalency whose balance is always shifting. Creation is transformed into Creator, sub-ject into object, immanence into transcendence, but only so that all can be as it first was, and now is: shifting and shimmering.

Person

There seems to be a real need in us to think of Jesus as the Cosmic Christ, just as there is a real need to think of Mary as the Cosmic Mother haloed by the stars. The exigent desire in us to see this way comes back again and again, across time and culture. It is important to attend to this urgency. If imagination insistently relays these images, then they must be part of the very fabric of personhood. The poet, above all, must attend and care deeply for what continues to come back over a lifetime of writing. Much can be lost. Perhaps most everything can be lost, but some things are not lost precisely because they are not ours to loose. When we truly attend to the human person we perforce attend also to these given vitalities of our imagination—they are ways of seeing that cannot be let go of if we are to see at all. For me they go all the way through the commands of language. Let me pay attention to these inner imperatives before I get lost in the vicissitudes of my own private life. The Cosmic Christ and the Divine Mother are not dogmatic accounts of religious triumph, but are heuristic openings inside myself, leading me through the mystery of personhood—mine and yours.

> The fisher of persons
> does not conquer
>
> but waits in a boat for what rises

"Into All Crevices of My World"

Love can do all but raise the Dead
I doubt if even that
From such a giant were withheld
Were flesh equivalent

— Emily Dickinson

Love equivalent to the flesh. This implies an if/then equation: *if* love were equivalent to the flesh *then* we might see death differently. Those accomplished in this unity of flesh and love, go on, past present fathoming, as persons—*where resurrections be.* This metaphysical equation is born out of a potent visceral dream. The dream works hard at its mirror-equation, even though it is helplessly past figuring. You know how it is when you wake from a dream and feel, in your struggle with the angel of all mystery, you got an answer, but, waking, you no longer know what that answer is. You can't even elucidate the problem. We are distracted, as Dickinson says later in her poem. The daylight gives us disparate details that seem to scatter, even as we look at them. The scattering seems equal to the distraction. Our attention is taken, and then, as Dickinson relates, it is too late to realize whatever it was we had a chance to realize. And yet it seems so simple—*love equivalent to the flesh*—so basic to our humanity. Through this equivalency we ought, it seems, to be here in a new way, or at least be moving in a new direction. What goes on?

What *in the world* (or out of it) goes on? Distraction/concentration—perhaps both turn one into the other. It is odd that the mind, in its avowal—its *plea*—for unity, keeps going out and spreading itself and doesn't often seem to come back. Something more than the mind brings us back—it is personhood that returns us to our bodies.

> What
> do they think they will attain
> by their ships
> that death has not
> already given
> them? Their ships
> should be directed
> inward upon

Inward upon what? In the body of William Carlos Williams' later poems I sense a groping forward and shifting back. The above quote traces the poet's faltering gait with heartrending honesty. Inward upon what if not love's measure itself: the variable foot whereby we all struggle to walk as persons. Why do I return, decade after decade, to these late poems of Williams? They are humble and awkward and endlessly beautiful. They are like listening to Casals and saying: *it doesn't seem that hard; it is an old love, resonating with the cello's body. It is just Casals being himself.* Of course it is difficult beyond belief. And yet I believe it: love equivalent to the flesh.

The Limits of Guilt

Karl Jaspers holds fast to the notion that guilt is endemic to our finitude. Guilt does not just arise from an ethical situation, but is part of our ontological situation. Cognitive, emotional, and physical limitations do not alone give sufficient reason for primordial guilt rooted in my very finite being. These limitations are combined with another factor: I sense, inside myself, even as I am aware of my limits, a potential energy that exceeds them. What is this energy that I tap only in my small way? It is not just *my* energy, but is rather a power bequeathed to me from a universal source. Perhaps my guilt is that I do not access what is freely given.

Perhaps ontological guilt—as opposed to the ethical guilt of doing some personal wrong—is the flip side of despair. Nikos Kazantzakis writes that, "only beyond absolute despair is the door of absolute hope found." This sounds acutely existential, sounds like Kierkegaard standing at the birthplace of modern consciousness. The guilt is that we should somehow be other than we are, and this other is right here in us, and yet somehow we cannot grasp it. Here, I feel, the ethical problem is the ontological problem. Ethical wrong reflects—and comes from—ontological finitude: if my personal good was complete—was one with my very existence—what wrong could I commit?

Kazantzakis writes that, "our duty is to transform the moment into eternity." This seems to go hand in hand with his imperative that we transubstantiate matter into spirit. Transubstantiation, for Thomas Aquinas, is where the substance changes while the appearance stays the same. Perhaps in that crucial flash-point where absolute despair becomes absolute hope we see the world for a moment as transubstantiated: it *looks* the same, but we feel that something has profoundly changed. I wonder if here transubstantiation might be reconfigured via philosophical idealism. I sense the world materially while at the same moment *acutely* sensing—by an act of inner apprehension—that the world is all spirit. The transubstantiation, in other words, occurs in me. Sometimes we are so heavy with the thingness of things, whose acuity is all acquisitive desire, that we cannot experience this inner transubstantiation, this depth of realization. Perhaps in failure our guilt returns, but guilt goes hand-in-hand with possibility. I do not traffic with a poetics of hopelessness, where only action is vital, because action is primordial hope made manifest. Poetic action is hope made manifest.

14

Active Intuition

Active intuition: this is Nishida Kitarō's idea of sensual creation that informs the person. This is not an aspect of us, but our whole being—it runs from making coffee to making a master work of art. My friend James Pitt says that art is not about pure talent. Rather, art is focused on the work at hand, the ongoing work that never ends. In the focus of praxis—the effort that runs the gamut of any given life—we are not really involved in an explicit subject/object dichotomy, yet we *are* involved in a prehensive whole. Dichotomies, like person/world, or efficient cause/material cause, are reflexive and always come after the fact. With active intuition there is one work, and this work is the person herself. The person pours across any open space. The quiddity (or essence, or definition) of the person is in the quick of the quotidian. Essence is spread across—and even (perhaps) to some measure dissipated by—the endless idio-syncrasies of you and me.

The urgency of Nishida's active intuition exceeds his writing about it, just as the force of orality—or art work—exceeds any literate mapping of that force. Active intuition comes before the endless philosophical texts that try to reconnect, as by a kind of logical surgery, subject and object. Severing — or re-severing!—seems incipient in this literate explication of the problem. One might say that the problem comes about *through* its explication! Dichotomized writing that claims to seek unity bears at its heart the very severing it so earnestly fights against. Active intuition pours past this con-undrum because its energy comes before it. Active intuition is not arguing about such things. There is no polemic because no mending is needed. There is no conceptualized distinction between hand and earth. Say rather: earth shapes the hand and the hand shapes the earth. We *know* both, but we experience something else. It is all active intuition, and yet I don't always, or even often, know this. It seems that when I seek to know it I don't know it very well. I have to get back into the work—the quick of the poem. The intelligence of active intuition is only in the on-going work.

15

Poetic Epistemology

Here is a brief description of what Robert Sokolowski calls "identity theory." The mental image acts as a kind of lens leading the perceiver back to the palpable object in the world. There is, in other words, a real relation between the world we walk through and our mental apprehension of this world. The danger in identity theory comes when we slip into thinking that this relationship is so unequivocal— so univocal—that we grasp, through the mental image-lens, the object in its entirety, we understand it thoroughly. This, of course, is never the case. What we get is real, but it is never really everything. Our understanding is the subject of expansive wonder. This is especially true when what we try to embrace mentally is another person. You have probably heard someone say something like this: *Oh, I figured him out a long time ago.* In fact, I don't think we ever really "figure" anyone out.

Representational theory offers us a different epistemological approach. Here the mental image is less a lens leading us back to to the living world, and more a confected thing that may have an equivocal relationship to the world-object. According to representational theory, we are companioned by these image-things. Image-things are what constitute our world—we have no free access to the noumena, the thing-in-itself. The problem with representational theory is that there is a slippery slope from philosophical agnosticism into philosophical atheism. If the thing-in-itself is empty of all access, then why not say it is empty of all conceptual content. The mind is a sealed frame.

I don't experience the world in this way. The mind seems to be spread *out there* in the world. (I confess outright the poetry of this, and admit no recourse to proof.) The "sealed frame" idea seems to be an exclusively philosophical confection that had its inception in early Cartesian thought. The salient revelation of Phenomenology (for me) is the idea that conversation presupposes a living world. The world is what we talk about and build upon long before we start self-consciously to think about epistemology. Language is a trial-and-error work built upon the given ground that is all around us. This is the experience of any child.

Maybe the truth lies somewhere between identity theory and representational theory. We get to the world because the eyes of the world are already within us, but we also develop image-things that are exclusively ours. Whose to say that these image-things-become-symbols don't have their own powerful veracity, their own divine thrust. The symbol bears the heat of an inner meaning that did not come exclusively from the world. When image becomes symbol, its relationship to the world may indeed be equivocal. Inner mystery is not entirely resolved into outer mystery.

Or is it? "Mental Things alone are Real," wrote Blake. This is not true unless the whole world is a palpably mental—or mentally palpable—thing. So even representational theory leads us back to the world, albeit a transformed world, a world seen as charged with intelligence. Parmenides said that being and the thought of being are one. He may be right in ways we cannot yet understand.

The point for poetry, it seems to me, is that both theories live in language, and language lives only as it streams out like the chartreuse tendrils of the winter willow. We find ourselves tangled in language, and as we find ourselves we find also that these two understandings of thought stream through one another.

16

"I See The Tree With Lights In It"

We don't live in the idea of humanity, but in the company of real individual human beings. And yet our ability to abstract, and to traffic mentally within abstractions—if somehow taken nakedly, as if apprehended for the first time—should shock us. There is a strangeness to this, an immateriality which, while relying on the individual for its alpha and omega, its vital ground, seems to go elsewhere. To traffic in essences is to enter another dimension. What is this dimension?

A philosopher of Thomist persuasions will say that God's very essence is to exist. For God essence is existence. Thomism says this in a rather frank, matter of fact way—it is reduced to a question of logic. If every existent thing is radically contingent, and yet is sustained in its existence, then there must be a kind of existence, a divine sustainer if you will, that is by nature un-contingent: this Being's very essence *is* to exist. What is left out of the flat equation is the philosophically inexpressible and overwhelming mystery of this: *it is pure poetry*. Everywhere existence becomes a palpable idea only when it is grasped via a material being. But here existence is palpable *in itself*. How in the world can we give image to this? The poetry is salient because it breaks from all our renderings. The poetry is real because it leaps from the prow of the ship into unknown waters. (The poet knows she could not have leaped unless there was a word-ship—a worship—to begin with.)

Let me redouble the mystery: if we grasp conceptually a given existent thing through the categorizations of essence

—*this is a tree, that is a person*—then where essence is existence, essence must somehow also exist. This is to say that naked thoughts are, in a godly way, palpable just as existence itself is divinely palpable. What in the world is this *Realm-out-of-no-realm-that-cuts-through-all-realms?*

Where all trees are the Tree of Life, where thoughts float out, where roots float up and mix with pendent tendrils, a tree can be a person, and we can see with with another's— or with the Other's—saintly eyes. This is the beatific mystery right here with us. *I am the vine and you are the branches*, says Jesus. This is the existential Tree whose very essence is to exist. This is the Tree with lights in it. This is the Tree whose leaves are all eyes.

"Being and the Thought of Being are One"

There are perhaps two ways to read the Parmenidean equation. The first way goes with a strict economy between being and thought, both resolved into one created quotidian. Here I sense a clear problem: when thought finds its limit, being finds a like limit; when thought is dying, being becomes moribund—both are caught in the same Idealist quicksand. The second way claims that finite cognition is rooted in a vast Conception that both nurtures and exponentially exceeds it. To use Nishida Kitarō's word, being is always "being-in" the Greater-Other. This second way allows us to maintain the equation. By a curious turn, being and the thought of being remain one precisely because we don't know all the tendrils of thought. We don't know altogether what thinking is, and so we don't know altogether what being is. By a kind of apophatic slant the link between them is maintained. We are still in the quick of interconnective activity—the yin/yang of thinking-being. We are saved by what surpasses us. The intelligible flame is both reflective and prehensive. Alpha-mind is omega-being.

Ontic / Ontologic

For Raimon Panikkar, again

The violinist is supremely focused, in a zone far beyond simply reading the notes. The living presence of the music is his presence, indeed his physical presence. The entire symphony is concentrated within his own playing—body-mind-violin. This is an *ontic* understanding: the concentration is individual and microcosmic and complete.

The conductor is aware of the whole orchestra spread out in a half-circle before her. She is aware of the great complexity of this: each instrument needs to be drawn out and brought forward into one miraculous harmony. She hears the whole of being's melodic body arrayed in all its manifest limbs. This is an *ontological* understanding. The concentration is macrocosmic and moves throughout entire sounding of the symphony.

Can the conductor's focus also be *onticly* understood? Of course, indeed it must be. It is not only her waving wand, but her whole body that becomes the music—in this she is like the violinist. She also *is* the music, but her activated, listening body cannot lose the reach of sweeping orchestration, the catholicity of the composition, pouring through all its parts. So ontic and ontologic understandings pour through one another. It is within this streaming of one-in-many and many-in-one that the music is realized.

Further, it is within this unity of personal concentration and orchestral complexity that the music goes on, even after the instruments are packed up. The ontic act is sustained in the sparking hearth of fiery ontology. The orchestral fire is sustained through the ontic act of living flame, of human—and therefore personal—inspiration. The poetry goes on. Poetry is not, after-all, about a particular enduring composition, still less—God Knows—about being a well known person of letters. *That* kind of music never lasts very long at all. What lasts is love as the music of the spheres...well, not even this. What lasts is the music that plays far past our conception of cosmos. Even in this, even in this ontic reality is not lost. Personhood is still present, singing through the great reaches of the silence. It is you and it is me who keep the music going, and who go on in the music.

19

Paradiso, *Canto V*

For Pat Hinnebusch

In the dark green pool, ringed with stones, I watch goldfish rise, drawn by my presence, which marks their hope for food. They broach the surface, and the water shimmers. Through them the depth is given form. But the depth they came from is as real as their rising.

I am with Dante watching beings lift from an unplumbable well. Closer, they become persons, and call out to us: "Here is one who will increase our love." Presence is fomented by human increment.

At some chthonic level, the manifest conversation becomes one flow. Being is a transitive verb and cannot be inscribed by genus nor delineated even by a Dantean genius. Flow, dart, and dissolve—the vision of the depth is as liquid as the depth itself. Perhaps atheism is finally a denial of limit, of some unchanging arc that is above changing reality like a hard outline. The atheist directs his thought from transcendence to immanence. If he talks at all about the sacred, it is pitched to a present pulse. We are drawn down, we are drawn to utmost intimacy, an intimacy for whom every conception is mere limit.

It is this utter closeness that I return and return to as to a kind of Silence that allows for all loving conversation. Maybe the autonomous personal soul would not be such a needed concept were it not that we long to meet our loved ones, perhaps even more acutely after they have died. (I try to pay attention: I listen to this refrain of need within need in me; I take its intractable hollow gravely.) From these mixing deeps, from this bewildering concatenation, may persons rise to meet us again as from some "world not world but that which is not-world," as Eliot writes in the *Four Quartets*. It is the depth itself, out of love for us, that would allow this to happen. It is as if the depth might say: *Yes, those familial connections will be re-manifested for you, you can embrace again each beloved member, but then they shall with limpidity go again— as you too shall inexorably go—into pure intimacy.*

Intimate relationship precedes subject. The subject is the brief convergence of a myriad of relationships. This realization is heady, epiphanic, life-changing. Perforce it enters into theology, for God is bright-ranging and complete interconnectivity. God is eternally generate, eternally new at every instant. Creation is the constant verb of this eternally generate God. Thus creation is also, mysteriously, ever-new: a quick concatenation of leaping intimacies. This pure intimacy is now, even now, passing through autonomy. Personhood is all that surrounds any given person, interpenetrates her and goes out and out, flowing with all verbal being. So the definition of person changes as it engages with all of life. So the chthonic depth is cosmos itself, or meta-cosmos, beyond and within us.

20

Alpha, Beta, Gamma, Delta ...

In his book, *God Has Many Names,* John Hick maps out three ways, three possible approaches to interfaith communication. The first way is that one particular faith-approach has the fullness of truth, the circumscription of the whole truth. If you are not one with this same circumscription, then what you have to offer me is at best illusory and at worst down right evil. This first way is: *My way or the high-way.* The second way is a kind of ameliorated version of the first. Here the interfaith communicator might say: *Yes, there is some truth in what you offer, but it is at best partial—a kind of rivulet that runs from the reservoir of the whole truth, which I am offering to you.* This *sounds* better, but it is in fact not much more than a mollified version of the first way. For the third interfaith approach, let me extemporize from something the philosopher and theologian Raimon Panikkar suggests. If Sacred Being is the alpha and the omega (as the *Gospel of John* suggests) then this implies that Sacred Being is alpha, beta, gamma, delta, all the way through to omega. My epiphany, my faith-realization—or even my theophany, if you will— may be only at the point beta. What is of immense importance is that a non-Christian, say a Hindu or a Buddhist, may have revelations of sacred reality that center on gamma or delta. These revelations are not only *just* as authentic as mine —and this is the true bewildering beauty of interfaith communication—but they may as well be spiritual understandings that I have had no experience of at all. In other words, the ground of this third way is that you have something utterly real and deeply unique to offer me that I can get from no place save from you. There is a ranging multiplicity to the kingdom of God. To start from a position of spiritual privilege is at once to destroy this communion—and I use the word *communion* here with deepest gravity.

Poetry help me here. Poetry, help me out.

Communion flames up to be a sharing of the heart—a sacramental sharing of the very essence of life. The central sacrament of the Roman Catholic faith is the eucharist, but if eucharist marks the whole of the Christ-nature, marks, in effect, the whole of the Creator (and so by consequence the whole of creation living in that heartbeat) then how can the church limit its reception to those exclusively *in the know*? How could the church *know* into whose heart God wants to go —into whose heart God-work implicitly goes on? This is one example—just one example among many—of problems with spiritual exclusivity. We cannot know where the wind of the spirit will blow. The limits are ours alone, but the kingdom of God breaks limits and sees itself, radically, in the *other*, in the one who is not delimited by this or that given tradition.

Poetry must help me here. Poetry, help me.

I am a spiritual socialist. (Well, not just a spiritual socialist.) There is a metonymic relationship between my room and the world-community. You may need my books more than me, and I may need your books. You may need my words more than I can conceive, and I may likewise need yours. I may find your words to be food and drink; and I may find, in eating and drinking your words, that I have been starving for a long time.

21

Re-membering

You walk past the restaurant where you had dinner last night with friends. It was such a good night, the conversation so intense, so shared. It was as if the faces of friends were manifest from their very words, bodies and the gestures of bodies from the act of literate communion. It was as if (and yes) acute communion came first and gave birth to all present, and not the reverse.

There is another sense to this remembered night. It is the unshakable feeling that you and your companions should still be there. Passing the restaurant in the morning, it is as if you should still see everyone there—including yourself— at the now empty table. It should still be going on: a dream-speech as real as the morning you walk through. You cannot seem to let go of this feeling. What does it mean?

There is a strangeness to consciousness, and the strangeness is that we are never quite at home in time. The rigor of temporal causality—that last night gave birth to this morning and this morning will give birth to afternoon—seems somehow suspect. Something in consciousness belies time. David Hume's deconstruction of metaphysical causality here rings with a curious authenticity: consciousness is never quite at home in temporal causality. Consciousness is at its heart tempiturnal—it doesn't exclusively exist in time. Hence the mind's bewilderment when it finds itself subject to the vicissitudes and confusions of change. We do not just flow with Heraclitus, but are also held by Parmenides. The river goes on, but it is all One water, one perfect presence that gives birth to ourselves.

Anamnesis is the core of the poet, and the poet is the heart of the person. The oration of the poem reveals language to be a living act experienced now. Symbol is the ember of myth; and the symbol, blown upon in the act of speaking, makes the myth flare up. We live within it, not again, as by a kind of caused recall, but by a current clarification—an intensification—of the present. We are here. We are here in this shared consciousness, in this many-tongued literate mind.

22

Pax Poetics

"I have made a question of myself," writes Augustine, and here I must begin.

Unless King Lear had become, at least for a spell, a beggar, he would not have understood, even partially, the plight of the poor and homeless. He had, in the palpable way of hunger and cold, to own up to his own myopia, his own fault. Religious, political, cultural, and personal faults cannot be whitewashed. The whitewash always comes off. What we have done can become some kind of grace only when we do this crucial work of admission. When we do this work, then and only then can the blood which we have caused to be shed by the 'other' become salving, become a part of our own healing. In essence then the wound which we have caused becomes experienced as our own wound.

Perichoresis: dwelling within one another. How does one accomplish *perichoresis*? Already I have missed it by thinking it an accomplishment. The will's draw is final causality. We think of it as *out there*, we are working *toward* it. But whatever unity is it must be here or nowhere. If we are drawn by a final cause then we are drawn into the present, we are drawn *within*. If the proximate cause is praxis, the final cause is most intimate to it. Indeed the proximate cause would not lovingly work at all unless the final cause were not already present as its heartbeat. The final cause is oneness, is unity. It is clearly not here. It is clearly here. In this paradox I make a question of myself.

I cannot execrate the 'other' when I realize that the other is just as much a walking question as I am, and we both walk lamely. We dwell within one another in the limping question. *Perichoresis*. I try to hold to this without letting it be narrowed through any reductive definition. (Our brokenness is the breakage of definition.) I don't so much hold on to anything, but try and let the patterns return. Try and let deep patterns accrue in you and you. Pay attention to what comes back and comes back. Friends within one another. Bodies in minds. Through divine evolution perhaps intrinsic nature does not exist, but intrinsic existence does exist. Perhaps my mind will not be right until I realize—by a shock to the whole thinking system—that my mind is not my own. The illusory rigors of self and other are language based. And yet poetry—intrinsic existence—breaks across us like a wave. How to see that all along it has really not been breaking across us, but has been rushing through us. More: that we are the motes of its motion.

23

Returning To A Nascent Place

The desire for an ultimate Good is rooted within a psychological need for stability, for some unchanging sense in a life of nothing but change. This reach toward such a sense of the Good is an aspect of our psychic survival. This seems true to me; it seems an honest accounting of who we are as persons. But if someone were to say that, *because* our reach toward the Good is psychologically grounded, a notion of the Good-in-itself is fictitious, is nothing but a psychological construct, then clearly a logical error has been committed. Just because an idea, or even a dream, is entirely rooted in the issue of psychic survival, does not imply—still less prove—that the object of such a dream or idea couldn't be real. Psychological structures or biological complexes do not preclude the potential reality of any ideational object under consideration. The Good-in-itself cannot be disproved through such an argument, but then neither can the Good-in-itself be proved through pointing out the logical flaw.

So then where do we find ourselves? I think we are found in a nascent place where such need begins to be shaped. This is the place where the poem begins.

Yeats writes that rhetoric is "the will attempting to do the work of the imagination." There can surely then be a rhetoric to bad philosophy, where a predetermined will drives the facts over the edge of their own usefulness. There is also a rhetoric to bad poetry, where the will drives the poem to a safe and predetermined end. In good philosophy as in good poetry, we sense the imagination given free range for its discoveries and creations. In both, the nascent place is not behind us, but ahead of us. Bad poetry gives us judgements that narrow—or even cancel—deep proclivities within the person. Good poetry, like good philosophy, gives us wonder upon wonder.

I think of George Oppen as a very good poet. His Objectivism is rooted in Phenomenology, where the objective world is received in language. We really do have an experience of the world through our words, and this experience itself is the continual wonder of Oppen's poetry. This approach is substantially different from that found in language poetry, where the referent to language remains equivocal. Here relationships are intra-linguistic: poetry is a conversation about its own language; words converse with words in their own space. Things, of course, become quickly murky when theory meets practice. Rae Armantrout, as a progenitor of language poetry, seems to me equally an objectivist, caught up in the questions of the received world. Her starkly delineated image-relationships are about the strangeness of the mind-world relationship.

What is received and what is imposed? In Buddhist philosophy, attention rests squarely on contingency, on the radical concatenation, the fluid interdependency of all reality, be it mental or physical. For the Buddhist philosopher, to posit a sustaining substratum beneath all change is to shift attention toward the realm of essences, or forms, that survive and exist apart from mutating bodies. This is thought of not as a received understanding, but an imposed confection. Stay with the first reception, says the Buddhist, stay with the nascent perception that Phenomenology first gives you. This is the world, and this is the world given to us again in the interconnectivity of language.

The difficulty here is that language also—and perpetually—gives us universals. Language constantly abstracts from the particular; that is how it works—that is why communication works. Great poetry, by some miracle, lives in a state of in-between-ness—between the universal and the particular, or between the mutable and the immutable. Dante, in canto 31 of the *Purgatorio*, sees—reflected in the eyes of Beatrice—the image of a griffin shifting back and forth between creature (the lion-nature of the griffin) and divine being (the eagle-nature). And yet all the while—Dante tells us—the griffin remains whole in itself. In itself both natures are completely one. In the eyes of the beloved we see the shiftings of the contingent and the un-contingent, and yet all the while we know there is but one Good. This is one of many nascent places in the *Comedy*, and that it comes nearly three-quarters of the way into it seems important to me. We meet the nascent place while we are on the way.

24

Dogmatic Truth, Revisited

Where a theological dogma arises from an acutely experienced theophany, a philosophical dogma arises from a careful attention to logic. A philosophical dogma might be the principle of non-contradiction: a thing cannot be and not be under the same term and at the same time. A person cannot, for example, be sitting in a chair and sprinting the hundred yard dash at the same time. What about a theological dogma? A good example might be the God-showing of Exodus, the I AM of the burning bush. Out of this theophany the theologian develops a dogma: God is omnipotent and omniscient. Here we have a theological ground of certitude: upon this unchanging Is all further existence is predicated.

Both of these instances quickly become complicated.

There is a danger that arises when a philosophical dogma becomes a kind of imperial stamp, a Platonic mark of absolute certitude. Let me go back to the principle of non-contradiction. The principle may work in the arena of pure logic, where A = A is mathematically eidetic, but what about in the existential realm of the person? The person who aches to run, but is physically impaired, may realize running in an acutely imaginative way that far surpasses the jogger who has just passed her window. Love is sometimes most intensely realized when the lover is separated from the act of being with the beloved. So the principle of non-contradiction becomes murky and incomplete when subject to the vicissitudes of real flesh and blood experience. The principle is at best an opening in understanding that leads to further questions, and perhaps to further revelations. The openings we experience are always openings-along-the-way.

What about my example of a theological dogma? The theophanic I AM of Exodus which becomes the omnipotent God, without cause and without beginning or end, is also a provisional opening in understanding. The dogma arises out of questing-reflection upon the theophany, and leads to a flux of further questions. How does this uncreated existence relate to our own existence? If the I AM is all, then are we nothing? Is the I AM-affirmation somehow within us as the barrier-breaking spirit of our lives? Is this spirit autonomous-to-itself, or is this I AM-spirit the very essence of sharing such that it has no life outside of relationship? If so, does this alter our sense of the un-predicated power of the I AM? Or is nothing lost when the I AM is resolved into such ongoing intimacies?

These are the kinds of questions born out of any theological opening-along-the-way, born out of any theophany. A particular truth—be it philosophical or theological—does not function alone, but has efficacy only as it figures into a questing process. Those who love philosophical-theology find, over a lifetime, that it is often not the answers that seem, in the end, full of intelligence, but the very questions themselves.

25

The Apologetic Limit

As a branch of theology, apologetics looks into the circle of a given religious system and seeks to tighten and clarify its meanings. It seeks, above all, to defend these meanings as they are defined within the circle. Theology, taken more expansively, looks outside the circle for meanings and relationships. Great theology, like the Holy Spirit itself, breaks boundaries and seeks an embrace of the other, even as the other remains resolute in its otherness. The essence of great theology is spiritual courage. Its faith is that, if the Good is really the Good, then nothing is really lost. Outer quest is predicated upon this inner trust.

I understand the need for apologetics, the need for definition, integration, and defense. I do not understand—or give ascent to—apologetics when it is equated with the deepest of theological work. And yet I often see, in my own local church, that those books deemed most worthy, most *catholic*, are, first and last, apologetic. Catholic means *universal*, and I take this most explicitly. I don't mean, by catholic, that my circle is taken and applied like a trans-parency upon every other circle I find. I mean by catholic that what is universal exceeds my understanding. What ever the truth is, it surpasses me hugely. Work, creativity, vision, take place within this surpassing light.

Aquinas wrote that truth is the adequation of object to idea. Let me take the object here to be goodness, manifest in whatever way the world offers it to me. My *idea* of the good is always in relationship to this manifest good, is always challenged and changed by it. Clearly, this adequation is not easy. It involves a poetic and boundary-breaking struggle. It is a work not without fear. The spirit of theology does not say: *I got this forever right in my inner circle and it's not going to change at all.* The spirit of theology says: *I struggle with that Thomistic adequation daily as it works poetically and pliantly in all the world.*

26

Pluralism

Is the tower of Babel myth strictly a story of hubris, of the overweening reach of the elite to achieve the power and knowledge of God? Raimon Panikkar has a different take on the myth. The error revealed by the story is not simply the will to conquer, but rather the will of an artificially confected homogeneous humanity. The Babel myth says: humans are automatons directed toward one political or spiritual goal. There is only one totalitarian spire we all aspire to. Counter to this, Panikkar proposes that pluralism is our ineradicable condition. Integration can only occur within, and by virtue of, pluralism. We meet the other as a *you*, a divinely unique messenger.

There is the sense in Panikkar's thought that history needs multiple divine incarnations, everyday theophanies, new realizations of God. These incarnations are plural, and this presents a real challenge. But perhaps spirituality is first and last about challenges, and consequent changes that take place within a given person. This process can be as idiosyncratic, as *personal*, as any of us are.

The personal soul has often been understood as an integrating principal that in-forms a given person. This integration is both inner-ordering and outer-gathering. What does the soul integrate if not the cosmos as it is humanly experienced. But the act of integration occurs differently in each of us. If there is a certain universality to these acts of integration—if we note patterns and derivations from patterns—it is because they are particularly rendered. The challenge is in meeting both of these—the universal and the particular—in such a way that we do not reduce them to a kind of homogeneous entropy, but rather find a dynamic equipoise between the two. Union comes about through the honor and respect of difference. I think poetry leads the way in this. Great poetry has always been leaps and bounds ahead of the political climate within which it was written. It draws from a deeper, and more spiritually radical, spring-source. We are taken by poetry—as *ourselves*—into new contacts, new emergent events, new peopled presences.

27

One To One

Lovely, lovely woman, let
me sing, one to
one to one, and let
me follow

— Robert Creeley

I have always loved the way Robert Creeley lets the poem
break down to its pure rhythm. There is a kind of exultation
to this—a joy in the naked dance—even as it is reduced to its
abstract numbers. Indeed, the joy breathes from this pulsing
essence of the poem. Creeley may have received this sense of
dancing number from William Carlos Williams:

Putting

their feet down
one before the other
one two

one two they
pause sometimes before
a store window

The image—what is in the store window—arises from the
peripatetic movement of the poem. What is pictured is given
within this movement. Image is inculcated into measure.

I think here also of Aquinas, pacing back and forth while working on his *Disputed Questions On Truth*. His pace, which I imagine as slow and considered—like a walking meditation— becomes the careful oration. (Aquinas did, in fact, dictate his work to a scribe—his pace was in labor and gave birth to the words.) For me it is not so much that Aquinas gave the 'right' answers—his answers are always provisional, and sometimes wrong. The issue—the meaning—is in the fluxing measure—the variable foot—of the questions themselves. Indeed, Aquinas' counter arguments, which he refutes along the way, most often seem to be seeded with their own truth. Where is the balance between idea and object? Where is the truth? I cannot help but think of Aquinas as a poet, whose working-walk is moment by moment, one to one to one.

Let me end *Poetic Faith* with a little poem of mine.

> Leah said: *when I fall in love*
> *it will not be because*
> *it is a man before me*
> *or a woman*
>
> *It will be*
> *that such love carries me*
> *to the beloved, one*
> *to one*

SOURCES

Robert Duncan

> *The Collected Early Poems and Plays*
> University of California Press, 2012

> *The Collected Later Poems and Plays*
> University of California Press, 2014

> *Collected Essays and Other Prose*
> University of California Press, 2014

Arthur C. Danto

> *Beyond the Brillo Box: The Visual Arts in the*
> *Post-Historical Present*
> University of California Press, 1992

John D. Caputo

> *Heidegger and Aquinas*
> Fordham University Press, 1982

Thomas Aquinas

> *Disputed Questions On Truth*
> (Translated by Robert Mulligan)
> Henry Regnery Company, 1952

> *Basic Writings*
> Random House, 1945

Current Thomistic thought:
Norris Clarke

> *Person and Being*
> Marquette University Press, 2004

Karl Jaspers

>*Philosophy (Volumes 1, 2, and 3)*
>(Translated by E. B. Ashton)
>University of Chicago Press, 1969

>*Truth and Symbol*
>Twayne Publishers, 1959

Nishida Kitarō

>*An Inquiry Into The Good*
>Yale University Press, 1990

Robert E. Carter

>*The Nothingness Beyond God:*
>*An Introduction to the Philosophy of Nishida Kitarō*
>Paragon Press, 1997

Dōgen

>*Treasury of the True Dharma Eye*
>Shambhala, 2010

>*The Zen Poetry of Dōgen*
>(Translated by Steve Heine)
>Dharma Communications, 2005

Kazuaki Tanahashi

>*The Heart Sutra*
>Shambhala, 2014

Dante

>*The Divine Comedy*
>(Translation and commentary in six volumes by
>Charles Singleton)
>Princeton University Press, 1975

Raimon Panikkar

       Opera Omnia: Volume IV,
       Hinduism: The Vedic Experience
       Orbis Books, 2015

       The Rhythm of Being
       Orbis Books, 2010

       The Cosmotheandric Experience
       Orbis Books, 1993

       Opera Omnia: Volume VI
       Cultures and Religions in Dialogue
       Orbis Books, 2018

A.H. Coxon

       The Fragments of Parmenides
       (Translations by Richard McKirahan)
       Parmenides Press, 2009

Perry-Schmidt-Leukel

       Religious Pluralism and Interreligious Theology
       Orbis Books, 2017

John Hick

       God Has Many Names
       The Westminster Press, 1982

Immanuel Kant

       Groundwork of the Metaphysic of Morals
       (Translated by H.J. Paton)
       Harper Perennial, 1964

Robert Lax

>   *Poems (1962 – 1997)*
>   Wave Books, 2013

Emily Dickinson

>   *The Poems of Emily Dickinson*
>   (Three volumes edited by R. W. Franklin)
>   Belknap, Harvard, 1998

William Carlos Williams

>   *The Collected Poems of William Carlos Williams*
>   Volumes 1 and 2
>   New Directions, 2001

Nikos Kazantzakis

>   *The Saviors of God*
>   (Translated and with an introduction by Kimon Friar)
>   Simon and Schuster, 1960

Robert Sokolowski

>   *The Phenomenology of the Human Person*
>   Cambridge University Press, 2008

>   *An Introduction to Phenomenology*
>   Cambridge University Press, 2000

Ron Silliman

>   *Ironwood 20*
>   *Realism: An Anthology of 'Language' Poets*
>   Ironwood, 1982

Robert Creeley

The Collected Poems of Robert Creeley, 1945 – 1975
University of California Press, 1982

The Collected Poems of Robert Creeley, 1975 – 2005
University of California Press, 2006

ABOUT THE AUTHOR

David Mutschlecner grew up in Bloomington, Indiana; moved to Santa Fe, New Mexico, in his mid-twenties, attending graduate school at St. John's College; and has called New Mexico home for over twenty years. He is the author of four books of poetry, all published by Ahsahta Press: *Esse*, *Sign*, *Enigma and Light*, and *Icon*.

☽

Drift Gestures (2023)
C. S. Mills

El Creacionismo (2022)
Vicente Huidobro, trans. by Jonathan Simkins

Goslings to Prophecy (2021)
Anne Waldman x Emma Gomis

Marrow Music (2020)
Nick Hranilovich

Bruised Gospel (2020)
Sarah Alcaide-Escue

Morning Rites (2019)
Reed Bye

Poetic Faith (2019)
David Mutschlecner

Printed in the USA
CPSIA information can be obtained
at www.ICGtesting.com
LVHW042359250724
786543LV00004B/70